Frogs That Sing And Others

Frogs That Sing And Others

poems by
Joan McIntosh

abbott press®
A DIVISION OF WRITER'S DIGEST

Frogs That Sing And Others

Copyright © 2012 by Joan McIntosh.

All rights reserved. No part of this book may be used or reproduced by any means, graphic, electronic, or mechanical, including photocopying, recording, taping or by any information storage retrieval system without the written permission of the publisher except in the case of brief quotations embodied in critical articles and reviews.

ISBN: 978-1-4582-0555-1 (e)
ISBN: 978-1-4582-0556-8 (sc)

Library of Congress Control Number: 2012914238

Abbott Press books may be ordered through booksellers or by contacting:

Abbott Press
1663 Liberty Drive
Bloomington, IN 47403
www.abbottpress.com
Phone: 1-866-697-5310

Because of the dynamic nature of the Internet, any web addresses or links contained in this book may have changed since publication and may no longer be valid. The views expressed in this work are solely those of the author and do not necessarily reflect the views of the publisher, and the publisher hereby disclaims any responsibility for them.

Any people depicted in stock imagery provided by Thinkstock are models, and such images are being used for illustrative purposes only.

Certain stock imagery © Thinkstock.

Printed in the United States of America

Abbott Press rev. date: 08/14/12

for MAC
and for my dear family and friends
and for friends I have not yet met

Acknowledgements

"*My Lives*" and "*Dream Bells*" were both published with Honorable Mention by Passager in their 2009 annual poetry contest issue.

Other poetry books by Joan McIntosh:

Branch and Shadow Branch	1982
Lake Michigan Shore	1997
Greatest Hits	2001
Walking Amazed	2002
Dancing the Kiss	2006

Contents

Part I: Here
    A Good Life 2
    Early One Morning 3
    Wind or No Wind 4
    My Apology 5
    A She-Turtle's Afternoon 6
    The Yellow-headed Blackbird 7
    Finial On The Fence Post 8
    Wild Cats Near Our Apartment 9
    Who Is Nice? 10
    Shrike On The Fence 11
    Three Worlds 12
    Frogs That Sing And Others 13

Part II: There
    Spring At Your Northern Wisconsin Summer Home 16
    An Unfamiliar Road 17
    Far Away 18
    Dream Bells 19
    Searching for the Scene 20
    Our New Sky 21
    Helicopter 22
    When Did They Know? 23
    My Lives 24

Part III: Then
    My Mother's Birthday 28
    The Beach At Grandma's Cabin 29
    Phone Call To Ginny 30
    The Distance 31
    Time Of The Wildwood 32
    My Mother The Sculptor 33
    Rainbow 34
    Meditation 35

Part IV: Now

Eighty-fifth Birthday 38
Ironing 39
Paying Bills At My Sunroom Desk 40
For All These Times 41
A Visit to the Art Gallery 42
These Days A Restlessness 43
Stuff 44
The Funeral 45
Silver 46
Sometimes It's Necessary 47
New Year's Eve 48
A Note To An Old Friend Up North 49
She Died Two Weeks Ago 50
Destinations 51
A Gift From Africa 52
They Ask: Who Is The Wind? 53
Tree Tunnel 54

Part V: Always

In Our Eighties Or It Ain't Over Till It's Over 58
Rituals 59
After Love 60
The Need to Be Lost 61
Wherever We Are 62
Shapes and Shadows 63
Sunrise 64
Forgive The Pencil 65
Hello Love 66
Days of Joy 67

Part I

Here

A Good Life

Seventeen white ibises proceed
in an orderly line around and
around the pond, thrust
their curved pink bills into
the slushy edge, pull out
delicacy after delicious delicacy,
occasionally rinsing mud away

before the gulp, and we can see
another animal's slow descent
inside each graceful neck. Then

by agreement they pause, wander
a short way from the pond,
arrange themselves equidistantly
on the lawn, with one as lookout,
and nap. After a nap, a bath,
and more circling, they gather
again, and in a graceful swoop

fly up and away to the roost
where they'll meet old friends
from everywhere for gossip,
chatter and finally, sleep.

Early One Morning

Two fat muscovy ducks
and two talkative mallards
converse in the middle
of the road, refusing
to move for a car.
Then three cattle egrets
slide through the air
to the edge of the pond
for breakfast. A pale
soft-shelled turtle,
large as a dinner plate,
paddles across the pond
with its flapper feet.
Four or five painted turtles
rest together on the shore.
We who live here call it
our pond.

Wind or No Wind

This day blue electric bright.
Not a twig dances.
Not a tree nods. The ocean
miles away with its mighty
pulsing. It doesn't know this kind
of stillness.

Sing trees!

And sweetly they do--a gentle
swaying with the kind push
of a soft wind.
A few vultures circle expectantly.
A human drives to the store.
In our small pond a merganser
dives for a fish.
The neighborhood red-shouldered
hawk waits on the fence
unmoving.
Its prey will come.
And the prey?
Yes, they too with pressing needs
wind or no wind.

My Apology

Each night, through the pines,
I see your pickup on the dirt road,
bumping toward a light
that must be your home. Our giant
obtrusive multi-storied retirement
community has smothered
your country world.
Now and then the few deer left
slip from your woods to sip water
from our artificial ponds then fade
back into the woods. Who else
is there, not daring to venture
to their former world?
A shy bird, a wary fox?
Our gaudy street lights melt
what was once a star-studded sky.

A She-Turtle's Afternoon

With her hind feet she scraped
a hole while she looked up
in the air, indifferent it seemed
to what was going on back there.
But the crows knew, they
gathered and spied, waiting
until she was ready.

Those eggs, those babies
to be, never had a chance.
As the turtle ejected eggs,
the crows grabbed them

and she kept gazing up.

Bright yolks splashed
on the grass. Crows grabbed
and gulped. She kept on laying,
though never programmed

to sit on them, help them hatch
or cherish them for life. But
somewhere a few will hatch,
survive and save the species
after another she-turtle finishes
and walks away when the crows
are full or busy elsewhere.

The Yellow-headed Blackbird

The day is wonderful and different
because a new bird, that is,
new to me, flew by across the pond,
above the trees, then disappeared.
But I saw its bright yellow head,
black body. What else could it be?
I'm too old to jump for joy but
I gasped then grabbed a bird book
to check on its behavior,
checked it off on my lifetime
list then wondered--is there any
wild animal that would jump,
hop or wiggle for joy if it saw us?

Finial On The Fence Post

The finial on the fence post
is a hawk, not stone, but silent
feathered flesh. A vole
ventures out and the last it knows
is a shadow, a slash of talons.
There is music too—a wren
singing, a woodpecker drumming
on a dead branch. And
a blossoming dogwood tree.
Perhaps the wren will find a mate
and the woodpecker hear
an answering drum. Just now
in the slowly brightening sky
a blue heron rows past my window.

No soldier of the morning news
sprawls limp and bleeding here,
only an opossum dead near the
road. A vulture's shadow slides
across the pines. Now sun fills
the air between the trees and lights
the needle-strewn forest floor
as the vulture's cousins
swirl to the roadside kill.

Wild Cats Near Our Apartment

Two cats are lying on the grass
singing back and forth, and
sometimes, after long exchange
they stand, arch their backs,
shout nasty yeows, then back
to civilized discourse.
The black one is bibbed in white
with four white paws. The other
is mottled, tweedy, big eared.
Now the conversation has turned
sour. Black leaps at Tweedy
with a string of invective. Tweedy
snarls. They roll into the bushes.
It's almost time for the Doctor
who has befriended them
to arrive with two bowls of food.
They've gained weight with
his generosity but still eye him
and the rest of us suspiciously.
Yeow! they say.

Who Is Nice?

Are robins nice?
Are wasps nice?
Are wolves nice?
Do they ask if we are nice?

The lady robin sits on her
lovely eggs and waits.
Her mate brings her worms.
Do worms ask
if robins are nice?

A pack of wolves catches a deer.
A mud dauber wasp eats a spider.
We sit down to a steak dinner.

Shrike On The Fence

A shrike on the tennis fence
waits, immobile and sleek,
obliging while I focus binoculars.
He's formal in his black, white,
and grey, calm but alert
as he waits for prey he knows
will come. And he will grab
and stab with his tough bill
then impale each on a wire
or stick. He has family,
responsibilities to mate
and children. He provides
them with meals from saved
carcasses—an insect, a bit
of bird, a slice of mouse.

Three Worlds

Broad daylight when
an opossum trots by,
trots by quickly
toward the road, but
a car is coming.
The opossum reverses,
trots by again
back to the woods.
Why is a night creature
venturing out now?

Just as the opossum
disappears three men
and one woman enter
the tennis court just
beyond the possum's
trail. They start to play.
They live in our
retirement community.
They rest often.
Back and forth, back
and forth. Rest and chat.

Just beyond and high
above the players
in the tall pines two
red-shouldered hawks
light on a bare horizontal
branch. They sit quietly.
Suddenly the male mounts
the female. A few thrusts
and wiggles and off.
They sit some more
then one more time.

Frogs That Sing And Others

The words are pine, cypress,
oak, red-shouldered hawk, ibis,
snowy egret, bluebird, clover,
beetles, more beetles of every
color and size, great egret,
bees, humans, ants, turtles,
frogs that sing in the night,
deer, dogs, rats, cats. Who
is more important than who?
And who can answer?
Little Tommy Tucker
Sings for his supper.
And the ibis eats its way around
the pond. A tiny frog catches
a tiny fly. An ibis eats the frog.
Oh sorrow.
And Oh sweetness
as a yellow butterfly flutters
among us.

Part II

There

Spring At Your Northern Wisconsin Summer Home

You called me to say you'd arrived—
but something in your voice.
You don't sound like yourself, I said.
Mice, you said.
What? I said
Everywhere, you said. Mouse turds
in every drawer, all over the floors.
Oh my, I said. Have you caught them?
I asked. Two, only two, you said.
You sound tired, I said. I am, you said.
The mice got into the doorbell and
it rang all night. And it snowed ten inches.

An Unfamiliar Road

The deer was running for its life
but we didn't know that.
It leaped the fence.
We hit it on the low curve
of its flight. The dog pack
followed, crossed the road,
then milled around, confused.
But what do we do with a dead
deer on a strange road?
And a pickup stopped to answer
our perplexity.
Oh, we'll take it straight to
the conservation office they said.
We all smiled. They had knives
in their belts, guns in back.
We thanked them warmly.

Far Away

In that country
men say
that women cause
earthquakes
by not
covering their heads
as men say
they should.

And the defiant
few push
their head scarves
back, feel
the rumble
beneath their feet,
and pull them off
completely.

Dream Bells

I know a poem is not
a business proposition but,
last night, in the small village
of my dream, bells
were tolling from four
of the town's six churches.

What in heaven's name!
A friendly citizen smiled
at my wonder: our priests
and pastors rent out the bells

anytime but Sunday or
during funerals or marriages.
They ring for birthdays,
new babies, graduations,
anniversaries, even
some divorces. And,
she leaned in to whisper,

when the town clerk
married the mayor's ex-wife
the mayor paid for twelve
hours worth of ringing.
Three hours is seventy-nine
dollars. The day the team
won the championship

almost everyone chipped in
to ring all bells all night.
A few complained but
the priests and ministers
and the mayor too
only smiled benevolently.

Searching for the Scene

Yes, there's the intersection.
First the railroad track then
the sharp dip down to the
highway below. That's how
the paper described it.

There's
where she hit the railroad
and the train roared.

Today is light and clear.
Trees arch comfortably
over this back road. Horses
run within well kept fences.
She wouldn't have seen them
that night. It was so dark.

Our New Sky

Winter pale blue sky.
Thousands travelling
way up there, plane
streaks crisscrossing,
passengers walking
in those tubes in the sky.

How many years ago
was sky only sun,
and clouds and moon
and stars, a space
we couldn't enter.
Ancestors left
their countries
for this land, never
expecting to see
friends or family
again.

And here, today,
in Florida a friend
told me she is
dashing to a party
in San Francisco--

just for the weekend.

Helicopter

Helicopter time
again.
Medical transport
for some battered
soul lying up there
above us, nurses
leaning
over the body
whose eyes are
open, closed,
tearful, afraid
almost not alive.
The bright blue
morning matches
the blue and white
machine spinning
over us. We know
the route--southeast
to the hospital
roof. And somewhere
someone won't
arrive for a meeting
or morning coffee
And later
someone's phone
will ring.

When Did They Know?

In other places, now
and back then, when
did they know? When
do we learn it is time
to talk carefully, avoid
words that say
too much? What is
too much? When do
we learn to hear words
beneath official words?
When do we neighbors
start to wonder
about each other,
smile cautiously
in passing, wonder
if we can talk
about our fears?
When do we learn
to only nod if we meet
each other on the street?
When does darkness
close in? When
do we flee?

My Lives

I'm in another place, covered
by my burqa, a black shadow,
as I'm required to be, half blinded
by the narrow eye slit, slipping
along a wall of buildings.

I'm on another continent, lying
under a burning sun, gang raped
and stunned with a screaming
fire between my legs.

I'm in a distant place, crouching
behind a sofa, shaking with fear.
Explosions rock my city. Bitter smoke.

I'm here on a beautiful evening,
walking, breathing in sweet air.

I'm here, here. How am I here?

Part III

Then

My Mother's Birthday

One hundred and nine years ago
my grandma pushed her out.
It's hard to picture that tiny bundle
of squall becoming the stunning
woman she became, but then again
we all start with a squall.

Scientists studying baby squalls
have discovered that French
newborns have a French lilt
at the end of their scream
while German babies start
loudly and end abruptly. Nein!

Do we all resist our birthing?
When does amazement start
over this new place. Where
are we? Who are they?

The Beach At Grandma's Cabin

A wide sand beach stretching
from one far land point to the other
and only me between them.
I was twelve, maybe thirteen.
Here sweet stones, warm
and smooth. And there
a small stream trickling down
from higher ground, cutting
a shallow channel in the sand.
Perfect for bare feet. I ran, I leaped,
I jumped, I stopped to watch a gull.
Far out on the lake a ponderous
tanker pushed north. I was young,
alone, free. A girl on the beach.
Grandma was tucked in the cabin.
My parents were far away and I
not even wondering what comes next.

Phone Call To Ginny

I decide that this morning, now,
right now, I'll call you way up
there from way down here,
fly back seventy-six years
and we are nine, racing
across the street to Midgie's
or into your house for cookies
your mother just made or
to the vacant lot for baseball
with the rest of the gang.
What a life! Your voice
on the phone is as girlish
as mine. We are still nine
and giggling. No one is left
who knows what we know
of way back then. But we,
we know how to conjure
so all the old gang joins us.
Jimmy, Norma, Arthur,
Midgie, Doris, Dick—
Join us. Come!

The Distance

You—noisy, exuberant,
the organizer--
became a ghost
before you died,
became so quiet,
sitting
pale and mysterious,
at the edge
of a room, always
half-turned to a door,
watching us
from a great distance.
Pale, translucent and,
amazingly,
shy--not of us—
but of something
you were seeing,
something we couldn't
see and toward which
you were inexorably drawn.

JOAN MCINTOSH

Time Of The Wildwood

Beneath that apartment building,
the huge one on the corner,
roots of oaks, maples, poison ivy,
trillium squirm in remembrance
of what they were. And a girl,
now an old woman, remembers
too, skipping to that woods
from her house a block away,
then quietly, quietly walking
on its interlocking paths,
discovering a wood thrush,
a warbler, a new white flower.
She pauses, leans against
a well-remembered great oak.

My Mother The Sculptor

She gouges, chips, sands. And
there the great head, his lips,
his big infectious laugh,
his always gesturing hands.

Each log becomes a part
of who she is and who
he is. Married so many
years before he faded away.

In another log she finds
the lovers entwined. Wooden
arms and torsos transform
to embracing passionate flesh.

Now in a smaller piece,
he is much older, lowered eyes,
lips sad, longing for, but not
understanding, what he has lost.

But she understands and carves
and knows her loss. She
finishes this piece, then
puts her tools, finally, away.

Rainbow

If you see a complete rainbow,
all of it, from one side to the other,
arched for you, then bow to beauty,
delight that you are so honored.

For a few minutes it silences
the news— a starving child,
a broken soldier—the way
Beethoven's Ode to Joy, soaring
in a great hall, the musicians
giving their souls, makes us gasp.

I used to go to a small gallery
in the middle of Washington, D.C.
and sit in front of Renoir's
"Boating Party". And breathe.

Meditation

Two large thunderclaps
this morning early
awakened all
who weren't up
and doing.
First thunderstorm
of spring, lightning
sparking bare wet
branches.

My 1920's mother
in a stylish cloche
leans across the years,
shrugs her shoulders
with a smile, says
come on, get going.
I did it, you can too.
And the air turns
brighter.
Of course we die.

Part IV

Now

Eighty-fifth Birthday

"Tell me, what is it you plan to do
with your one wild and precious life."
Mary Oliver

What is it I plan to do? There's
no time for planning. Each minute
now is the doing. Breathe in the joy
of the child, this child, this great-
grandchild, mine, hugging me
then leaping into the pool. Breathe
out. Laugh. Breathe in the sorrow
of the daily news and shouldn't it
be mentioned first? The daily
sorrow. One person after another
with no time left for planning or
doing. Breathe in as I watch a bird,
an unknown bird circling the pond.
Breathe out joy as I look up its name.
Pink legs, red bill, black belly.

Ironing

This morning, pushing the iron
expertly across your best shirt,
I traveled smooth roads across
the plains, reached the Grand Canyon,
looked into its depths, wondered
again about all those who were born
and died thousands of years before us.
Born and died. Here. Then.

A spritz of starch.

And now
I'm on the slow boat to Wales
for a long reminiscence.
Then sitting in our cozy Welsh
kitchen near the Aga stove.

Spritz for a perfect collar.

The Welsh mountains loom
beyond our windows. And
a Welsh choir sings in four
part harmony. I keep on ironing.

Another spritz for a finish
on front panel, pocket and plaque.
There! Done! It looks good.

I'm home.

Paying Bills At My Sunroom Desk

I'm trying to concentrate but
two cypress trees across the pond
from my cluttered desk have colors
only an artist can duplicate: a dab
of rusty brown on the palette,
but more than rusty, a gleam

of red, a bit of yellow, a drop
of winter black, a dash of sky,
a glow. A wonder against dull oaks
and fading vines. This bill says
"overdue" with a threatening voice

as a vulture soars overhead—
a turkey vulture, not a black.
Funny, that helicopter over there
flies by each morning just about now
and who is that neighbor on the walk?

Four white ibises are carefully
working their way around the pond,
one by one. With each step they jab
their bills into the mud for whatever
morsel they can find. Walk Jab
Walk Jab Walk Jab...

For All These Times

Let the soup be as delicate
as the gently simmering carrots,
as definite as the bite of onion,
as quick as the pucker
from candied ginger and all
of these and more in a soothing
mix of creaminess, a sprinkle
of mint. The perfect meal
followed, oh yes, by love.

Or let it be white grape soup
with English cucumbers, chilled,
with cloves of garlic, green onions
and fresh dill. A long, delicate
recipe to construct and then
to admire and sip while we
talk and talk and now
dear friends one of you is gone
so I make this soup
in memory of our fulsome
conversations and serve it
on a summer's day like then.

Something boisterous now
with children, grandchildren
and great-grands. Sausage,
chicken, peppers red and green,
all in a broth with onions, garlic,
celery and cayenne. A noisy
soup and always someone's
birthday. Here comes the cake!

A Visit to the Art Gallery

The label says Triangles Within Rectangles.
I see rose-colored labyrinths, and a dancing
triangle of pale tan holding the angle
of another.
And this picture label says
Black and White with One Red Dot.
I step back. The red dot comes toward me,
larger, larger. I step toward it.
It leaps back onto a black streak and then
to another.
And now, back home,
I look down at the pond, an oblong
in a rectangle of green with small white
moving dots around it and a gray noise
hovering.

These Days A Restlessness

The birds can't seem
to settle down.

Cattle egrets,
snowy egrets circle
the pond, touch down,
rise, circle
the apartment,
circle the pond
again. One lands

on the tip of a tree,
teeters,

takes off,
continues circling.

Coarse voiced crows
won't stop their noise.
Something (but what?)
is going on.
I'm restless myself.
A great egret almost hits
my window, but rises

in time to circle the trees
again and again.

Stuff

First, old letters, then bits of paper—
jottings to help my memory,
receipts I didn't need to keep,
Christmas cards from six months ago,
all of these to read and toss.
Here's a letter written by a dear
friend two weeks before he died.
Family letters go
in the family letter file—
for my family to throw away later
when the time has come.

The Funeral

I've chosen not to attend.
Is it truly just three
weeks ago that we met
briefly in the mailroom.
We don't, we didn't
know each other well.
After our hellos she said
I'm getting so thin.
Do you think I should
see a doctor? Oh yes
I said. I think I would.
Then we parted
and never met again.

Silver

Silver a sliding sound,
S to L through V to R.
More than a tray,
a teapot, a silver spoon
but a silver night,
a silver star, a soft sound.
So why are hard objects
given the name?
Silver: I love, you love.
Silver the soft spring night.
Silver rustling.
Silver silence.

Sometimes It's Necessary

Sometimes it's necessary
to cast away words,
to be
that bluebird on the fence
or the gull careening
over the lake
in a west wind,
or become again
the young girl alone
on that empty beach,
sand between her toes.

New Year's Eve

Today the rains didn't come.
A TV announcer said they would
and the Weather Channel said
they would but the clouds
didn't hear and floated by.
The scummy pond kept shrinking.
No burning allowed, no
fireworks was the decree.
Celebrations were subdued.
But we stepped outside as usual
at the midnight hour
and we heard a defiant sound—
one pale firecracker said "pop!".

A Note To An Old Friend Up North

I don't want to bother you
with exclamations about the sun,
now half risen, nor the golden sky.
It's at your place too, nor about
tall pines swaying in the wind.
You've seen a pine or many pines,
nor about the deer over there
across the pond. I know you have
plenty of those although I'd like
to mention how these particular
young play and cavort. But no,
I won't. I'll put the dishes
in the dishwasher, sweep
the kitchen floor, wonder
what in my world I can tell you.

Joan McIntosh

She Died Two Weeks Ago

What do I say after "sorry"
and "is there anything I can do?"
I barely know you. If we meet
in the apartment hallway
I want to say "blueberries
are in season now" or
"have you seen the deer
across the pond?" or
"she is everywhere,
in everything you ever loved".

Destinations

At first it seems that a wind
an unexpected wind
is causing the grass blades
to quiver and shake
and then we see them--frogs--
hundreds of baby frogs--
no, thousands--hopping
up hill. We try to avoid them
as we walk down to the pond
but we have killing feet.
I'm sorry, I'm sorry I say
but they are only inches
apart, a siege of frogs
hanging on grass blades,
resting beneath them.
Where are they going?
For days we see splayed frogs
squashed on the road and
others, still alive, hopping
as we are walking
to our particular destinations.

A Gift From Africa

Is a clear sky here the same as
a clear sky in Africa?

This morning's early dream
was a giraffe walking slowly
around the small pond below
my third floor window.
Sleek and spotted handsome.
His head reached to my window.
I longed to stroke his flat fur neck
but the glass was between us.
I swear he was really there.
We looked at each other nose
to face. He tilted his head
and, yes, he smiled.
Awake, I see only a turtle
way down at the edge.
The large and muddy tracks
encircling the pond are the dream.

They Ask: Who Is The Wind?

There, across the pond
from my window the trees
are talking. They nod
and chatter, pause, consider
their next words. Their
relationship with the wind
is not always easy. Most
days they can gently bend
and talk together in easy
neighborliness. Last night
was different. The wind
turned wild, pushed them
against each other. They
crashed and cried in horror
and the pain of splitting
trunks, twisting,
grinding tree against tree.
Who are we? Who is Wind?
And why?

Tree Tunnel

Inside the tunnel of trees--
ash, maple, elm, oak, cherry--
is a world. Just to stroke
the varied bark takes the daily
headlines away. The tunnel
leads to a stream that gurgles,
sings like the music
of the Moldau my grandmother
played on that old wind-up victrola.

I hear highway cars far away.
Planes are miles high
in that other world of rush.
I watch a woodpecker,
listen to a distant wood thrush.
I can't bow out of that other
world but oh—the thrush
comes closer. A red-bellied woodpecker
makes its coarse, compelling call.

Part V

Always

In Our Eighties Or
It Ain't Over Till It's Over

What's different?
We eat together each day.
We read, we walk,
we meet with friends.
We talk and talk.
We laugh because yes,
you eyed, with every other
man, that slim, mincing
woman in six inch heels
and skin tight jeans
swiveling up and down
the supermarket aisles.
And we laugh because
yes, I love to watch
ballet dancers, male,
their wide leaps
and bulging tights.
And at night, cozy
in bed, we caress,
remember, sleep.

Rituals

The awakening, the stretch,
our early morning kiss,
a stretch again, the turn
half out, legs feeling free,
the quick walk, the pee,
the shower, sweet water
splashing, the soaping,
wiggling, rinsing, oh
how nice, the drying
minute by minute, blue
towel, dry between the toes.
Then lotion, combing hair,
sweet smells rubbed on.
The clothes. Minute by
minute. All in time. Count
one to sixty evenly if that
is what you need. Each
minute of the day
is a minute of the day.

After Love

If
fresh strawberries
follow
and
buttered
cinnamon toast
and
tea
isn't that
perfection?

The Need to Be Lost

Music sounding
along thousands,
yes, thousands
of years, cooing
to an infant, chanting,
a quiet drum
to mark the voices,
a louder drum, minor
and major chords
or one flute-like
bell-like tone.

Who invented soprano,
baritone, bass? When
did voices start to sing
in fine-tuned harmony?
Or many instruments
join together in
chords so spellbinding
that we, for a moment,
forget our raucous world.
Don't stop we cry.
Don't stop!

Wherever We Are

Wherever we are, even
quietly reading, or
sleeping, we are swaying
in the roll and swing
of the globe.
Don't you feel
this little third floor
apartment rocking gently
in the morning sun?

Shapes and Shadows

In this light that bush contains
a silhouette—there's the head,
a large head. See? It's a man
with hooded eyes, straight nose,
full lips and a head of curls
flowing to his shoulders.

We do this time and again.
Look, there's a mermaid
in that cloud, and that cloud
looks exactly like an elephant or
Napoleon or Elvis. But this time
he might be real. He might be

an ancient ancestor. He's so
distinct, more than an open mouth
crying, more than a cloudy Napoleon.
He wants to know what happened
afterwards. He wants
someone to remember his name.

Sunrise

The sky
stretched
spread
pink tendrils
south to north
and high
exploded
in fire.
What a show!
If we
took time
to stand
beneath it
every day
and marvel
what might
be different?

Forgive The Pencil

Forgive the pencil
for being unforgiving
not allowing
that truly stupid phrase
to desecrate the paper.
The pencil was right.
I was wrong.
And even now it pauses,
tells my fingers to relax,
not push the line.
Let the pencil say
what it needs to say—
the faint grayness in the sky,
blue as it is,
but a warning within it,
a serious warning.
Listen.
Watch.

Hello Love

Being this old doesn't mean
I can't stay awake and wonder
who you are and who I am
and how we have lived together
a long and for us amazing story.
And now it is slow dance time.
And isn't this the way
it should be. And isn't this
still our world to be amazed
about. And family to love.
Come!
We're alive until we are not.

Days of Joy

Days of joy yes there are such days
and who cannot rejoice a full sun
and hope and longing and young
couples along the street and
a single woman and a lone man
seeking and hoping to meet
and two men who love each other
and two women in love and we
older ones loving while the sun
bright bauble in the full sky
makes lonesome people feel
less lonesome and hope is a sweet
ribbon a never ending ribbon
floating between you and me
and you and you and we.
 Don't let go.